I0115739

How to Write Family Stories

Susan Williamson

HighTide

Publications, Inc.

Copyright © 2019 by Susan Williamson

Thank you for purchasing an authorized edition of *How to Write Family Stories*.

High Tide's mission is to find, encourage, promote, and publish the work of authors. We are a small, woman-owned enterprise that is dedicated to the author over 50. When you buy an authorized copy, you help us to bring their work to you. When you honor copyright law by not reproducing or scanning any part (in any form) without our written permission, you enable us to support authors, publish their work, and bring it to you to enjoy. We thank you for supporting our authors.

High Tide Publications, Inc.
Deltaville, Virginia 23043
www.HighTidePublications.com

Printed in the United States of America

First Edition

ISBN 978-1-945990-32-8

Edited by Cindy L. Freeman

"There was never yet an uninteresting life.
Inside the dullest exterior,
there is a drama,
a comedy,
a tragedy."

- Mark Twain

Contents

Why Before How

Why write family stories? Each of us may have a different reason and any reason is valid. Do you want to leave a legacy of how life was for those who follow you? Do you want to remember particular people who were notable in their accomplishments? Do you want to flesh out a genealogy by describing the appearance and character of the relatives you remember or even those who came before you?

Are you writing only for your family or do you have a fascinating bit of memoir which you think would make a best-selling book? Perhaps you are trying to gather stories from elderly relatives before they are gone.

Your purpose will help you decide what to include and how to organize your work. Your purpose may well change over time, once you begin the organizing and writing process.

A dear friend of mine wanted to make something for her grandson's wedding. A friend of hers told her, "You need to do something memorable and creative and very special."

"I know that," she said, "but what?"

"You're a good cook. What about a family recipe book?"

Once she started collecting and organizing recipes, she decided to include stories from her life and family with each section of recipes. Then she added pictures and scrapbooking details to build a wonderful recipe memoir.

One writer I know self-published five books about his life. His first book dealt with growing up on a farm in rural North Carolina. Each subsequent book described his life in different phases. He presented a program to our writers' group. His life was interesting but not extraordinary. His writing was clear and chronological, but not particularly creative. I wondered how his program would be perceived by an audience ranging from novice to successful published writers.

The group was most interested in, and some inspired by, his process and dedication. He devoted hours every day before going to work, to his writing. He wanted to chronicle his life for his children and other family members. I doubt that he sold many books, but that was not his purpose.

I wrote a nonfiction piece about my mother's bipolar disorder. It was a memoir, but my purpose was to shed more light on this issue and how it may have affected her life. I wondered, in retrospect, how many of the stories she shared with us were products of her manic behavior and how they may have been interpreted by those around her at the time.

When my youngest niece married, I wrote several pages about my mother, her grandmother, as a part of her wedding gift. I included the bi-polar issue, because the condition has a slight genetic propensity and because it was a part of who my mother was. I also wanted my niece to know that her grandmother was a beautiful woman who dressed in style, a generous hostess who loved celebrating holidays, and most of all, a fun and loving mother.

The point is, what you include is up to you. Think about your audience and what you want to tell them. You have the power to include or exclude anything you wish. If you have other living relatives, you may want to get their input on certain incidents or individuals or you may not—this is your project. If preserving a picture of life during a certain era is your goal, it is helpful to research media accounts, documentaries and other books set in the time period. If you have pictures, the technology of scanning makes it easy to include them.

For example, I have a picture of my father and his mother riding in a boardwalk cart in Atlantic City. I know it was taken after his father died and that he took his mother on a trip to the resort. I know the approximate year, and I could research what hotel rooms cost in that time period, what the city looked like, etc. In the picture, my grandmother looks young and stylish, which was remarkable considering she had raised eight children to adulthood, lost two in infancy and fed and housed numerous cousins during the worst of the depression. I never knew her, but there is no doubt in my mind that she was a remarkable woman. As I write this, I remember other things I heard from my father. My approach would be to write down everything I remember and then organize and edit what I want to include.

If you are planning to leave a family heirloom or a collection of items to a certain relative, you could write about each item's history: the people who owned it, its significance to them and so forth. You could write about a collection of say, teacups, by telling the story of how and where you purchased each one. You would in effect be writing vignettes about your life.

You might choose to write separate stories about individual relatives. Another option would be to tell only the family stories that occurred during your lifetime. You could also write them as creative non-fiction pieces to eventually become a collection.

Memory is not infallible. Your memory of an event might not be the same as someone else's, but it is your memory. However, if your memory is a total alternate universe, you may face criticism from family members or others who have their own versions.

There is no right or wrong way to go about recording your family history, but if you begin with a purpose, you will find it easier to decide on the content and organization.

Notes

Organize

Once you have decided why and for whom you are writing your stories, it is time to organize. You might want to gather pictures and mementos first. Sorting through family pictures may take some time. Hopefully someone has identified the subjects and possibly the year or occasion. If not, you may need to consult with relatives or friends.

Now think about the "why?" Are you after historical accuracy? If so, you may want to organize chronologically. Perhaps separate stories and pictures arranged by time periods—i.e. childhood, teenage years, early adulthood, etc.—or by decades.

Or is there an important event that will become the main focus? In that case, you may start with the event itself and then flesh it out with backstory and subsequent events. If you are writing stories about several family members, you may wish to spend a chapter or two on each, including stories which speak to a person's character, are humorous, or have an important role in your family history.

One writer I know is writing a family story by telling, as a narrator, facts which he has researched and interspersing them with fictional stories of the lives of his ancestors, based on what he has learned about them.

My friend who created the cookbook/memoir organized by type of food—appetizers, soups, main dishes, and so forth and then included family stories and pictures in each section.

Whoever your readers are, they will want some type of logical flow. I have read professionally published biographies as well as autobiographies in which the author skipped around so much that I ended up thoroughly confused and frustrated.

Initially, you may want to begin listing things you want to include and one idea may lead to another. If this is how you work best, by all means go for it. Write what comes to mind, but try to at least put different stories and people in separate paragraphs. The beauty of computer copy, cut and paste is that it is easy to write now and sort later. Remember to copy and paste before you cut so that you don't lose something important.

You could write a series of stories about different events and let each story be a chapter. "My Trip to the Circus," or "Grandma's Cookies" or "How my Mother Learned to Cook."

Another approach might be dividing by notable times: "Christmas on the Farm," "Summers at the Beach," "Baseball Days."

A workshop presenter I heard recently told his audience, "The last thing you do is write." Recording snippets and stories when they occur to you can help to jog your memory. Having an overall plan will help you decide what goes where. And remember, you can always change your plan.

What Pictures Say

Pictures are wonderful additions to family stories. If you have scanned and stored your photos on a computer, they can be added easily. If you scan them in black and white, this won't increase the cost significantly. Color pictures will of course cost more in ink and increase the cost of printing your manuscript. You may be able to scan a color picture in black and white.

If, however, you plan to self-publish or use a publisher, pictures, especially in color, can increase costs.

Clear, portrait-style pictures are a wonderful way to give more personality to your stories. You may also want to include graduation and wedding pictures or other event pictures. Informal snaps help to describe personalities. Depending on the age of the pictures, you may need to enlist the help of family members to identify subjects.

Living family members should be asked for permission to include their photos. And if a relative doesn't want a particular picture included, you should honor their wishes. Professional pictures from public events may have copyrights. For example, I have purchased many professional pictures from horse shows. If so, you should always ask permission from the photographer before including them in any printed materials.

Pictures of houses, city streets, gardens, vacation spots and so forth help set the time and place.

My parents faced many physical and mental health challenges in their sixties. I have some vivid and sad memories of those times. But

I also have a picture of them together, smiling at a steeplechase event. That picture tells me they still had happy times, and it makes me feel better. One of my favorite pictures of my grandfather was taken in the fall in the yard of our farmhouse. He wore tweeds in autumn shades and stood amidst brown grass and leafless trees. A weathered wooden fence can be seen in the background. The photo tells me he was in the autumn of his life, but very present in the moment.

Pictures of family picnics, reunions and dinners all help to connect us with who was alive and in contact at a certain time.

Newspaper stories and photos about our family members are also helpful. You may want to include articles about significant things that happened in the time and place you are writing about. My parents saved a New York Times edition from the day I was born. We saved a USA today from 9/11.

A poor quality picture will probably not add to your work. Sometimes a photographic studio can enhance an old picture. We had only a damaged baby picture of our adopted son, but I took it to a studio and they improved it enough to give me an acceptable baby picture to frame.

Your Memories are Real to You

Every person's memory is unique. You may remember an actual event or you may have heard it repeated so often in family stories that it seems real to you. Eyewitnesses to events often tell very different versions of the same story because everything we see and hear is filtered through our own experience.

To a small child, a loud noise, a tall person or a normal-sized room may seem enormous and overwhelming. I loved my mother deeply. She was fun and caring but she was also always an authority figure. She was less than 5'2" tall and weighed under 95 pounds. By the end of high school, I was two inches taller, but I never realized that until I was a junior in college. I would have never thought of her as petite, although she clearly was.

As children, we don't tend to question family stories. My mother talked about going to Denver to attend boarding school for a year because of her sinus problems. My grandmother drove her to Denver from Indiana–this would have been in 1930. Looking at it now, it seems an extreme action, and I can't help but wonder if there was more to the story. I wish I had thought to ask her sister while she was still alive.

I mention in the opening chapter that other family members may have very different memories. They may have been older or younger and understood more or less about what was happening. When you record your memories, you may want to acknowledge that not everyone agrees with your version of the story.

A memoir should be honest—as honest as you can make it. In other words, it should be your memories of actual events or people, but not imagined adventures. And although you may remember something differently than it actually occurred, be careful to do some research if it was a public event and there are other witnesses still living—some celebrities have been discredited when their version of events was proven false. And you don't have to include everything you know. Some stories might be boring or might portray you or others in a bad light—it is your choice whether to pass them along.

Some memories are funny and help to flesh out a person's character. My mother never bought any yellow clothing for herself nor for us and she never chose to paint a room yellow. When I was in eighth grade I bought my first dress on my own, a yellow cotton shirtwaist. My mother laughed and said she had never liked yellow since the time when she had her tonsils removed and she was wearing a yellow dress. I chose yellow for my bedroom when I was in high school, but once I left home, she repainted it.

My father told the story about the time that he and his brother hid in the rumble seat when his oldest brother went on a date. Once downtown, they extracted movie fare as the cost of giving the couple some privacy. My father had seven brothers and one sister. I can picture good-natured mischief in a house full of boys.

Neither of these stories is important, but they give personality and time-capsule glimpses. Rumble seat, for example, is not a common topic of conversation these days.

Stories from Others

Has someone on either side of your family ever written any family stories? You can include excerpts, as long as you give credit to the author.

Your relatives will no doubt know stories that you don't—whether you include them or not is up to you. Family members and close family friends can also provide different viewpoints on the stories you tell.

Instead of asking for family stories or memories in general, you might have better results by asking about a particular time period or recollections of a certain relative.

When I was growing up, my brother and my mother often teased my dad about the fiancée he had when he met my mother. He claimed that he was not engaged, he had merely given a friend his diamond stick pin to keep until the war was over. "But it was made into a ring," they would say.

Life is strange and it is indeed a small world. Many years after my parents had both passed away, a friend married a girl from McKeesport, PA, my father's home town. We were invited to our friend's Christmas party and since I had lived in McKeesport until I was six and had many relatives there, I asked his wife where she had lived. It turned out that her mother was upstairs babysitting. "You'll have to meet her," she said.

Her mother had grown up on Jenny Lind Street as had my father. When I told her that, she raved about the handsome Sullivan boys next door. As we talked, I realized I was talking to the girl who had the stick pin. Not wanting to open old wounds, I didn't ask for more details. I know she eventually married someone else, but what an opportunity I had to collect information.

I have read several good biographies based on collections of letters. What a treasure they can be.

One of my husband's cousins shared a letter that her mom had received from her brother, my husband's father. There was nothing of startling import in the letter, but it provided a nice snapshot into his life in the years before my husband was born. I wonder if our children save our emails as snapshots of our lives?

Both my husband and I have relatives who have done genealogy research, and if you have a large family, chances are some of your relatives have done research as well. You can use their information as background or a starting point.

Of course, you may find skeletons in the closet and once they have escaped they can be hard to put back. This reminds me of a funny story my mother told. When she and my father had first met, he was bemoaning the mess of his apartment and the fact that his brother was coming to visit. She volunteered to go clean for him. Knowing my mother—it must have been love at first sight because she hated to clean. Anyway, she opened a closet and a *real* skeleton fell out. My dad had been enrolled in medical school before the war.

Research the Time and Place

Sometimes a story is better understood if we know what was going on in the time and place in which it occurred. Thanks to the internet, such research is easier than ever. And, unfortunately, thanks to the internet, there may be many conflicting stories about events.

You can go to old newspapers available online or in local libraries. My mother told me about watching a lynching in her hometown of Marion, IN. I looked up the event and learned that two men were taken from the local jail and lynched. Her parents had heard the rumors and ordered their daughters to stay home, but they sneaked out, and I know my mother was sorry she witnessed the event. The actual newspaper photo appears with the article. I can't help but wonder if she was in the crowd in the picture.

Most cities and many smaller towns have interesting local histories. Reading these is another way to learn about the times. You may find that history books and newspaper articles have a different viewpoint than what your family stories say.

Through various genealogy sites, you can research census records. They list dates of birth and death and sometimes marriage dates, but they are often incomplete and an individual may show up in a subsequent census more or less than ten years in age difference from the previous census.

Without using any of the paid sites, I was able to find some interesting information. By Googling my grandfather's name, I found reference to an article about hotel managers in Indiana. If I had paid a newspaper research site, I could have read the article. I decided not to because I knew he was active in the Indiana Hotel Managers Association. The most interesting thing I found was listed on E-Bay. It was a laminated card with a picture of the Spencer Hotel in Marion, IN on the front and it said Alfred U. Thornburg, Manager. On the back was a quote about never giving up. And I believe that was a motto for his life until the end when he contracted tuberculosis. My mother claimed he could have recovered but no longer felt useful and finally gave up at the age of 84. I bought the card.

I decided to Google some of the other side of my family. I have a cousin who played football for Notre Dame. He was quite a bit older than I, so I wondered if he was still alive. I found a two-page obituary stating he had played professional football in Canada. I had heard that but didn't know if he really did. He died at the age of eighty and was known for his good sportsmanship. The obituary said he would take action if a parent was unruly at one of his children's or grand-children's sporting events.

In the above cases I researched by name. But names can be tricky. My father's name was Lawrence Herbert. All of my life, he signed his name L. Herbert Sullivan. But a picture from his Army Air Corp days bears a desk sign saying Herbert L. When I asked him about it, he said the army wouldn't use a first initial so he had to be Herbert L. A friend who did some genealogy research found him listed in census documents both ways (different years). My father's father was William Frances. He named his oldest sons, twins, William Frances and Frances William. The son of another brother was named William Frances II and his son William Frances either III or IV because by then my Uncle William had a late-in-life child whom he named William Frances. I knew these people and I can't keep it straight. Pity the future descendent who tries to write their story.

Then of course there is the whole issue of maiden, married and previously married names for women, not to mention women who keep their maiden names or whose children bear only the mother's name or a hyphenated combination.

Census takers may have misspelled names and individuals may have chosen to shorten or Anglicize their names over time. Some people are called by their nickname to the point where everyone involved may have forgotten their real name. Our adopted son was issued a new birth certificate when we adopted him at the age of seven showing our last name. He chose to be called by his former middle and last names in addition to ours. One family we knew had two sons named John but with different middle names.

Notes

Edit

Once you have completed your stories, it is time to look over the entire collection and do some editing. You may want to rearrange things in a more logical order. You may decide to omit some stories or add to others.

Read over your stories. Even better, read them out loud. That will help with your first edits. But nothing beats a fresh pair of eyes. When we critique our own work, we tend to see what we meant but not always what we actually wrote. The mind will substitute missing words and fail to notice "here" when we mean "hear."

If you are planning to publish your manuscript, find a critique group to help you polish your work. Often local writing organizations have critique groups. If you're not ready for a group, find a trusted but honest friend or family member who will read over your work and make suggestions. This is your work, so you don't have to use anyone's suggestions, but having others read it lets you know if it makes sense. You may have left out a word or punctuation which alters the meaning. Critique can be harsh, but valuable, so approach it as a learning experience, not a personal attack.

Is your significant other a possible reader? Spouses and children can be great proofreaders, but only if their comments won't put undue strain on your relationship. I never give my fiction to my husband until it is published. He doesn't tend to read mysteries or thrillers, and he is very literal. I do however consult him when I am writing letters to the editor or essays.

Be aware that the more people who read your work, the more suggestions you will have. Some of these will be helpful but many will not. So, choose wisely.

If you are seriously considering trying to market your book to a publisher, you may want to consider paying a professional editor.

To Publish or Not, For Few or Many

If you read the first chapter, hopefully you have decided why and for whom you are writing. Is it a few family members? A computer printing with scanned pictures may be enough. Perhaps an e-book is sufficient.

If your collection has more pictures than words, you may want to check out "Shutterfly" or a similar service which prints a picture book with words. Our daughter gifted us and other relatives with books of the first and second years of our granddaughter's life which needless to say were the best gifts, ever.

Self-publishing is easier than ever before. There are many options, but please do some research. Talk with someone who has self-published and look at his or her book. The most attractive and well done self-published books I have seen were produced by people who understood formatting and design. Sometimes the publisher will provide those services for a fee. Self-publishing or so-called vanity presses charge you to publish your work. There's nothing wrong with that but understand what you are getting. Print on demand allows you to order a small number of books, unlike the olden days when self-published authors ended up with 1500 copies in their garage. But remember, even if it is the best memoir ever written, the chances of getting your self-published book into a bookstore are very slim.

Small, independent publishers are another option. If a small publisher takes on your book, there will be no advance. You will be able to purchase books at a discounted rate and receive a percentage of the sales of any sold by Amazon or the publisher.

Selling to a major publisher is, like winning the lottery, always possible but not likely. Many publishers only buy manuscripts through agents. Others will accept works directly from the author. *Writer's Market* for the current year is a reference in your local library. Several writing magazines also list publishers and agents.

Whatever your reasons, researching and writing family stories can be fascinating and sometimes cathartic. Writing the stories of your ancestors and your immediate family can help you understand who you are and leave a legacy for those who follow.

About the Author

Horses, Mystery, and Travelare Susan Williamson's interests. She is a horse person, gardener, writer, and avid reader. She has worked as an extension agent, a newspaper editor, a community and adult education coordinator, the owner of a paint and wallpaper store, a riding instructor, trainer, barn manager, adjunct professor, and manager of a local farm-to-table coop. Currently she is writing, gardening and horsing around. The University of Kentucky and the University of California, Davis are her alma maters.

She met her husband at a horse show (after the horse she was riding ran away with her). Their daughter's first word was horse. She has been an avid mystery reader since she discovered Nancy Drew at the age of 9. Carolyn Hart, Rita Mae Brown, Nevada Barr, C.J. Box, Steve Berry, J.A. Jance, Sue Grafton and many more are her favorite authors.

She and her husband have recently downsized from 10 acres in North Carolina to a townhouse in Williamsburg, VA.

Books by Susan Williamson

Fiction:

Dead on the Trail
Tangled Tail
Desert Tail

Non Fiction

Buying Your First Horse - How to Make an Informed Decision
Getting by as Time Goes By
How to Write Family Stories

Children's Books

The Riding Lesson

www.ingramcontent.com/pod-product-compliance
Lightning Source LLC
Chambersburg PA
CBHW021344290326
41933CB00037B/724

* 9 7 8 1 9 4 5 9 9 0 3 2 8 *